SANTA BARBARA
GOLD

A PHOTO-ESSAY BY TOM TUTTLE

CREDITS:
Principal Photography & Design: Tom Tuttle
Contributing Photographer: Sandy Novak
Digital Project Editor: Tim Tuttle

PUBLISHED BY:
ShoreLine Press
P.O. Box 3562
Santa Barbara, CA 93130
805-687-8340
Fax 805-687-2514

DISTRIBUTED EXCLUSIVELY
TO THE TRADE BY:
Pacific Books
P.O. Box 3562
Santa Barbara, CA 93130
805-687-8340
Fax 805-687-2514

ISBN 1-885-375-05-0

PREFACE

Colors, shadows, sparkles, warmth, the wonders of nature, and the wonder of it all. My passion is the magic of light. Exploring and sharing the miracles of light keeps me entertained and makes me happy. My photographs are my sketches and notes. When I hold the camera up to my eye, I examine each element in the frame, using the viewfinder as a canvas for composition. Sometimes it takes a year or more to get the perfect light; other times it happens in an instant.

Digital imaging has created a new paradigm for my photography. I approach the computer as an exploratorium for the mind; a digital darkroom. It is a creative tool that empowers the imagination to take flight.

Viewing the world as a visual designer, I look for unity and simplicity, elegance and joy. Bringing it all together digitally, on film and video, has been my destiny; and it is now my pleasure to share these images with you.

Tom Tuttle
www.tomtuttle.com
Specializing in paradox, humor and change.

INTRODUCTION

One colorful word describes the most sought after commodity known to man. It is an element that denotes rarity, quality, luxury and eternity. It is a color that shines, glistens, blends, and outclasses every other hue of the rainbow.

It is the color gold. Gold can take any shape to suit its keeper, but the intrinsic value remains unchanging. It always *feels* the same.

The images that are captured by Tom Tuttle's intuitive eye, reflect Santa Barbara's palette of precious moments, dreams, and fantasies. Santa Barbara is a Golden place in the Golden State. A place where change is ongoing, but subtle; held dear by those who live here, who share a devotion to our Spanish/Mexican cultures that influence our architecture, cuisine, music and spirit that is our lifestyle.

The vibrant colors of this coastal city create a rainbow for the visitor's eye. The green-laden foothills rimming the endless blue Pacific Ocean, miles of white beaches and the silhouette of the necklace-like chain of Channel Islands . . . all under the umbrella of a crystal-blue sky dotted with great white clouds. What makes Santa Barbara's tapestry unique is the vivid echo of red tile roofs, her woven mat of brilliant flowers, stunning bougainvillea vines, and myriad species of foliage.

Combined, these colors form a fabric that creates a stunning backdrop for the residents and visitors of this unique town.

Slow of pace, ease of mind, the people who live and work here quickly learn to leave their memories of past lives behind. Never mind the frantic existence of Los Angeles, New York, Chicago, or San Francisco; here things take on the well known "Mañana Mentality". Everything will get done . . . in time.

One can relax in the hammock and do nothing, of course. But if you have the desire to get out, Santa Barbara is a town that offers everything any enthusiast could want. Water sports galore . . . sailing, power boats, fishing, surfing, canoeing, outriggers and personal watercraft are all available. Whale watching during the summer season is extraordinary; but should you miss the whales, there is an endless supply of playful dolphins that will surf the bow of your sail boat any time of year.

Golf and tennis are two of the most popular sports, but biking, hiking, and strolling the beaches are wonderful ways to take in Santa Barbara's sun-drenched air.

Cruise up and down State Street any day of the week. Walk under beautiful shade trees and sit awhile at one of the numerous sidewalk cafes, as you relax and decide which items you cannot live without. There are theaters, museums, galleries, and restaurants all within walking distance of each other.

At the end of State Street, the Dolphin Fountain marks where the continent ends and the ocean begins. Just beyond lies Stern's Wharf, extending another 2,000 feet offshore, where visitors can explore the ocean's secrets. The panoramic view of Santa Barbara from the wharf is extraordinary. One could just as well be in Southern France viewing the Riviera.

This intimate coastal village has to be one of the most fascinating cross-roads in the world. Many different languages can be heard, multi-cultural garb can be seen, and ethnic foods abound for the adventurous.

All of this is made possible by the sublime mediterranean climate. Santa Barbara is surely the Queen of Climate; the weather here is as close to perfection as one can find.

Those people who work in the film industry know of a special time of day referred to as the "Golden Hour". It is that time just before the sun sets . . . and everything takes on a golden glow. For some reason, Santa Barbara is blessed with an extra amount of "Golden Time" each day.

As you look at the images on the following pages you will find what many have searched for their entire life; the gold at the end of the rainbow. This special little town, Santa Barbara.

-Phil Behrens-

*"Santa Barbara isn't Heaven,
but it shares the same zip code."*

-Ronald Reagan-

Santa Barbara's jewel is the County Court House, surrounded by tropical gardens and adorned with a clock tower where visitors can get a 360 degree view of the city, mountains and ocean. Built in 1929, the elegant interior reflects the aesthetic of the era and the history of the city.

A Fourth of July picnic concert in the Courthouse Sunken Garden is an annual tradition for hundreds of Santa Barbara residents.

Founded in 1786 and built by the native Chumash Indians, the Santa Barbara Mission has
an epic past and is the last of the active Missions. It commands a breathtaking view and is
the most photographed spot in Santa Barbara.

Located in the center of downtown, Paseo Nuevo is an open-air boutique of restaurants, vendors, department stores, live music, theater and performances; occupying two city blocks.

La Arcada Court is a little Spanish courtyard with twinkling lights, flags, unique fountains and a variety of shops and restaurants. A large clock tower marks the entrance to this enchanting downtown landmark.

A series of whimsical, delightful and deceptively realistic sculptures, scattered in and around the La Arcada Court, wait patiently to be discovered. They were created by internationally renowned artist, Seward Johnson.

15

The well protected harbor is home to over 1,000 pleasure craft and commercial fishing boats. The magnificent campus of Santa Barbara City College looks down on the harbor and the city from its cliff side perch.

"Zen is being so present with whatever you are doing, that time is meaningless. You are not on the clock, you are on a roll."
-Anonymous-

Above: The "Harbour Queen" makes her way back to the Marina after one of her many daily sightseeing tours of the picturesque coastline as Lasers sail safely in the shelter of the harbor entrance.

Right: Color, joy, sunrises, sunsets, fog and fish. These are the lot of the Marina people. If one must live a life, it might as well be close to the sea where all life begins.

Stearns Wharf extends 2,000 feet beyond the end of State Street. There are restaurants, souvenir shops, ice cream, pelicans and fantastic views of the harbor and the city with a mantle of emerald mountains and blue sky.

A life size Gray Whale hangs in the entry to the Museum of Natural History's Sea Center located on Stearns Wharf. In addition to replicas of marine life, the Sea Center offers a living ocean bottom to enchanted children and their parents.

Above: Bring together some friends, torches, briquettes, food and song. Put them in the sand on a warm evening with a full moon, and you have a memory in the making.

Right: Family and friends bid a fond farewell to a couple who are leaving Santa Barbara. Of course anyone who has heard Hotel California, or has ever lived here and left, knows that you can check out - but you can never leave.

"Sometimes it's hard to avoid the happiness of others."
-Chris in the Morning-

Santa Barbara's front yard and playground. It is the kind of place that brings out the children in all of us. Fishing, swimming, walking or watching; all you have to do is show up to become part of the tapestry.

"When you realize that all your time is personal time,
you will do only those things that make you happy."
-Sandy Novak-

A bikini and a smile is the uniform
of the day for beach goers.

Above: The entire downtown waterfront is one long bike path. You can bring or rent a bike, skates, four-wheeled surrey or a scooter.

Left: This is how Santa Barbara kids spend their Summers and weekends. There is always something going on at the beach.

"*Grownups often accuse children of being dreamers,
instead of complimenting them.*"
-Anonymous-

It's amazing how serious grownups get about poking a rubber ball over a piece of string. It is something to do, it's good for the body, it's a darn good excuse to be at the beach; and if you aren't playing, it's just as much fun to watch.

Left: A swimmer competes in the regional championships at the 50-meter Los Banos Del Mar public pool, located on the beach between the harbor and the wharf.

Right: Water is synonymous with Santa Barbara life. Whether it's the ocean, a pool, or the fog that rolls in and out; it is virtually everywhere - always.

Above: A little girl's dream to be a beautiful dancer has become a reality for a day.

Right: Cancan girls (from the Santa Barbara Ballet Company) do the dance to the delight of the French Festival audience. One of several ethnic festivals held throughout the summer in Oak Park, visitors enjoy music, dancing, indigenous foods and special exhibits.

Above: For five days in July, Santa Barbara relives its historical past and Spanish heritage in a city-wide celebration of Old Spanish Days Fiesta. Parades, music, dancing, art shows, magaritas and Mexican food permeates the air.

Right: The children have their own version of the Fiesta Parade. Dressed in their finest colors and dancing up State Street to the music of children's bands.

The annual Summer Solstice
Parade occurs on the Summer
Equinox and brings out the crazy
creativeness of the whole town.
This is Santa Barbara's rendition
of the Mardi Gras and every bit
as colorful.

The County Bowl plays host to entertainment ranging from The Beach Boys to the Los Angeles Philharmonic Orchestra. Concerts are held in the evening under the stars.

That special day that students and their families mark their lives by. San Marcos High School is typical of a small town school. Little babies that grew up too fast, heads filled with big dreams and nervous anticipation of what life will be like tomorrow morning.

Hundreds of artists and school kids create wonderful chalk drawings in front of the Mission each year at the annual *I Modonnari* Italian Street Painting Festival.

The Farmers Market is a local meeting place on Saturday mornings. A rainbow of fresh fruit, vegetables and cut flowers creates a cornucopia of plenty, grown and sold by Santa Barbarans. High spirited professional musicians make shopping for groceries an unforgettable experience.

Left: The annual National Horse Show is one of the nation's premier events, held at the Earl Warren Showgrounds in July.

Above: Polo is big in Santa Barbara. It's not uncommon to see Hollywood personalities and even royalty in the stands on Sunday afternoons throughout the summer months.

Above: The Zoo brings out the kid in everyone. There are lions, tigers, elephants, giraffes, gorillas and a huge number of smaller furry creatures to fascinate everyone for the entire day.

Right: Kid's World is a fantasy playground created as a space "just for children" to play downtown. It was conceived, designed, financed and constructed by volunteers and local companies who came together to serve the little people; and admission is only a squeal or a giggle.

Outdoor cafes pepper the downtown area with aromas to die for and almost all of the more than 400 restaurants have outdoor seating. Food just tastes better outside, especially when it is spiced with fresh ocean breezes.

The Santa Barbara Museum of Art displays works of the great masters of the 18th, 19th and 20th centuries, along with special international exhibits. It also features a delightful children's gallery, gift shop and cafe.

Left: The Paradise Cafe says it all. One of the many terrific indoor-outdoor restaurants to be found downtown; off State Street, but only a block or two away.

Right: When the lights come on in the evening, State Street takes on a special glow of excitement. In the distance, off-shore oil rigs twinkle magically after the sun sets.

Above: The Lobero Theater, built originally as an opera house in 1873, is now home to the Santa Barbara Chamber Orchestra, Santa Barbara Grand Opera, and a variety of internationally recognized performances.

Right: The entrance to the Arlington Theater offers a warm familiar feeling of anticipation. The Arlington is an international performance venue, including the Santa Barbara Symphony, and a first-run movie theater. The interior is designed as a Spanish village with balconies and a star-studded sky on the ceiling.

Only the locals and keen sighted visitors are aware of the cobalt vases above the old Presidio Studios.

The exquisite ambiance of the Meridian Studios draws serious artists and art buyers from around the world. Once through the gates, it is a colorful microcosm unto itself.

Left: The Blue Angels make an appearance at the annual Air Show. The Santa Barbara airport is a joy to fly in and out of. It is often said, that one of the nicest things about leaving Santa Barbara is flying back in.

Right: Goleta, ten miles north of town, is the home of UC Santa Barbara and a rapidly growing number of high-tech firms. Circon, a world leader in miniature video cameras, constructed this magnificent Spanish building for their headquarters.

*"There are no gates to heaven other
than the ones we build."*
-Anonymous-

The Andre Clark Bird Refuge holds a reflection of the Monticito Country Club, mountains and palms trees. All threads of the scenic tapestry that weaves this coastal community into one of unending beauty.

"*The mind is everything; what you think you become.*"
-Buddha-

Santa Barbara is recognized worldwide as a playground for the rich and famous. Many of them have climbed these tower steps at the exclusive Biltmore Hotel in Montecito.

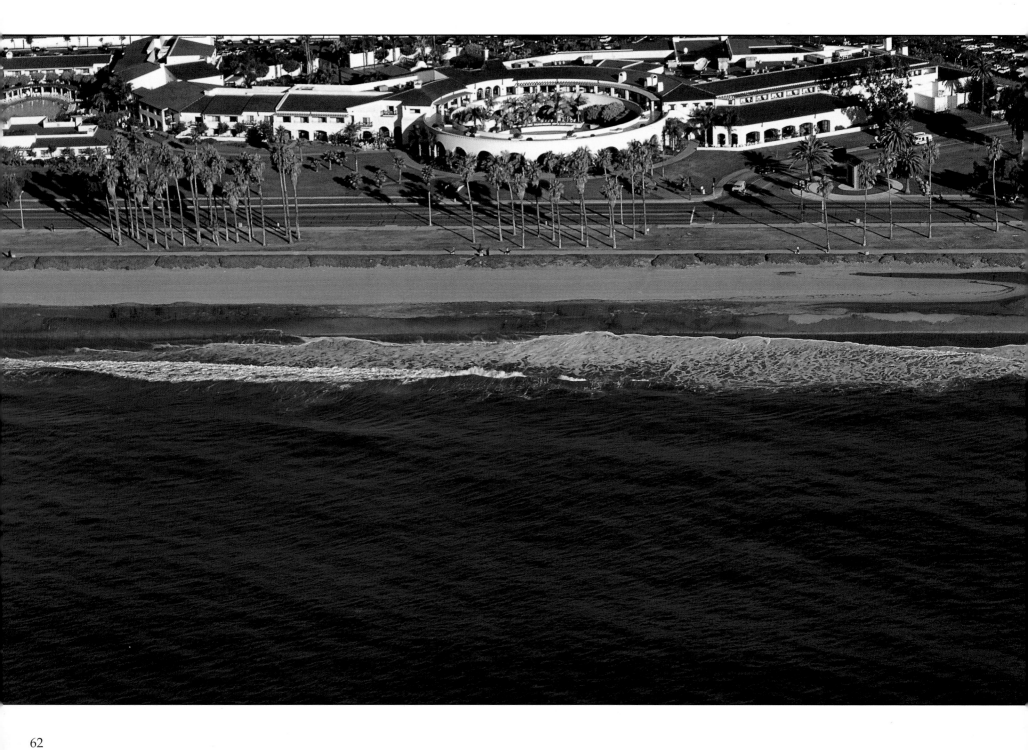

Left: Fess Parker's (aka: Daniel Boone) DoubleTree Inn commands the views that all know and love as Santa Barbara. From the three story rotunda skywalk, one can see a 360 degree view of palms, beaches, coastline, mountains and the wharf.

Above: Looking down from the skywalk into the rotunda, an international conference banquet takes on a kaleidoscopic panorama of color.

Left: As the ocean plane rises up the foothills towards the mountains, South facing homes get an ever expanding view of the city and ocean below. This area is know as the Riviera and its inhabitants can see the sun rise and set from their balconies.

Above: The Santa Barbara Historical Museum is an adobe structure housing the area's history in artifacts, photographs, books and maps. The picturesque courtyard is available to private groups to dine under the stars.

An aerial view of Hope Ranch is the only way to glimpse one of the most luxurious residential neighborhoods in the world. Miles of horse trails wind around magnificent estates nestled in the woods and perched on cliffs overlooking the Pacific.

Montecito is one of the most beautiful, most exclusive and most expensive neighborhoods in the entire world. Historically, it has been home to some of Hollywood's biggest stars, a summer retreat for royal families and a place where "heir" is a common and respected profession.

Left: As an international resort destination, Santa Barbara has become a year round golf mecca. There are PGA, public and several par-three courses to choose from. Usually uncrowded and always in superior condition.

Right: Designed by internationally renowned artist Herbert Bayer, the Chromatic Gate is a colorful landmark that radiates in the sunlight in front of the DoubleTree Inn.

Above: Santa Barbara City College, offering spectacular views of the city, mountains and ocean, is one of the premier colleges in the nation.

Right: More than twenty thousand students attend UC Santa Barbara's sprawling campus. It is situated on a jetty of land that is almost considered an island, with ocean on three sides.

Left: On Alisal Road, between Solvang and Highway 101, lies Nojoqui (pronounced: no-ho-key) Park. Studded with oaks and elfin forests, the park is a hidden away oasis of birds, streams, and well-equipped recreational facilities.

Right: Nearly 15,000 acres and twenty five wineries produce some of the finest grapes in the world, due largely in part to the unique weather found in the inland valleys. Cool moist nights and dry sunny days is the year round weather report.

A twilight country concert at the vineyard is a summertime tradition that brings this and many other families together in the Santa Ynez Valley.

Wine lovers from all over Southern California come to Santa Barbara's county wine festivals to - what else? - eat, drink and be merry.

EmmyLou Harris is one of many international stars that come to Santa Barbara's wine country to perform at Gainey Vineyard's Summer Concerts under the stars. The concerts begin just as the full moon rises over the vineyard. Visitors are encouraged to "partake of the grape" in the wine tasting room before the music begins.

Above: La Purisma Mission looks like it did in the 18th century; mules, dirt floors and all. It is open daily for tours and there is almost always a group of grade schoolers following a monk around the historic park.

Right: Imagine a valley filled with a breathtaking panorama of flowers that go as far as the eye can see in every direction. The floral display occurs from Spring through mid-Summer.

Three generations of Santa Barbara ladies snag a passerby to capture their moment of joy, while on a Sunday afternoon stroll in the Mission rose garden.

"Learn to wish that everything will come to pass exactly as it does."
-Epictetus-

"Love is infinite as there is no way to measure it. You may therefore have as much love in your life as you choose. You will get exactly as much love as you give; no more, no less, and you must give it first. That's the way love works."
-T Tuttle-

Right: A non-traditional couple having a traditional ceremony in an untraditional setting. After all, the beach is for a lot more than swimming and volleyball.
Shalom.

An old fashioned carousel is the centerpiece of the Chase Palm Park.

"Seeing isn't believing.
Believing is seeing."
-Kris Kringle-

Miniature Icelandic ponies are one of an ever growing variety of exotic livestock found in the Santa Ynez Valley. Don't be surprised to see zebra, ostrich, watutsi long horn cattle and even giraffes on a Sunday drive.

Girls and horses just go together. There seems to be a silent understanding of acceptance and gentleness that creates a mutual trust.

"You will see your self reflected in your pictures."
-T Tuttle-

Photography is about surfaces and reflections. We don't actually see the things in the world; we see color and light reflected from the things. The direction and intensity of the light creates texture and form in our three dimensional world.

"Life is simply an attitude.
The better your attitude, the better your life.
That's the way it works. You can count on it."
-T Tuttle-

The dolphin fountain is the most popular rendezvous spot for visitors. It was created in 1982 by the internationally known, and local man about town, artist Bud Bottoms.

Fishermen leave before sunrise, when the sea is calm. Sailors, by contrast, set sail in the afternoon when the winds pick up. Santa Barbara is steeped in the history of sailing and it is visible everywhere.

"One day at a time, one moment at a time. Live to the highest daily.
This is the path to living happily ever after."
-Swami Dayananda-